Library of
Davidson College

Library of
Davidson College

The Thomas Jefferson Center Foundation

The Pentagon's Office of International Security Affairs, 1969-1973
or
Two Citizens Go to Washington

Richard A. Ware

The G. Warren Nutter Lectures in Political Economy

The G. Warren Nutter Lectures in Political Economy

The G. Warren Nutter Lectures in Political Economy have been instituted to honor the memory of the late Professor Nutter, to encourage scholarly interest in the range of topics to which he devoted his career, and to provide his students and associates an additional contact with each other and with the rising generation of scholars.

At the time of his death in January 1979, G. Warren Nutter was director of the Thomas Jefferson Center Foundation, adjunct scholar of the American Enterprise Institute, director of AEI's James Madison Center, a member of advisory groups at both the Hoover Institution and The Citadel, and Paul Goodloe McIntire Professor of Economics at the University of Virginia.

Professor Nutter made notable contributions to price theory, the assessment of monopoly and competition, the study of the Soviet economy, and the economics of defense and foreign policy. He earned his Ph.D. degree at the University of Chicago. In 1957 he joined with James M. Buchanan to establish the Thomas Jefferson Center for Studies in Political Economy at the University of Virginia. In 1967 he established the Thomas Jefferson Center Foundation as a separate entity but with similar objectives of supporting scholarly work and graduate study in political economy and holding conferences of economists from the United States and both Western and Eastern Europe. He served during the 1960s as director of the Thomas Jefferson Center and chairman of the Department of Economics at the University of Virginia and, from 1969 to 1973, as assistant secretary of defense for international security affairs.

Richard A. Ware delivered the twelfth G. Warren Nutter Lecture at the American Enterprise Institute for Public Policy Research, Washington, D.C., on January 22, 1986. Earlier lectures were delivered by William F. Ford, Lawrence S. Eagleburger, Roger E. Shields, Paul Craig Roberts, Yuan-li Wu, James M. Buchanan, Thomas H. Moorer, George J. Stigler, R. H. Coase, Milton Friedman, and S. Herbert Frankel.

Additional copies of these lectures may be obtained from
the American Enterprise Institute
1150 Seventeenth Street, N.W.
Washington, D.C. 20036

The Pentagon's Office of International Security Affairs, 1969-1973 or Two Citizens Go to Washington

Richard A. Ware

Richard Anderson Ware has been associated with Earhart Foundation (and also Relm Foundation, 1951–1973), Ann Arbor, Michigan, since 1951. He currently is president emeritus and a trustee. In 1969–1970 he served as principal deputy secretary of defense (international security affairs) and then as consultant to assistant secretary Nutter through 1972. Prior to his career as a foundation manager Mr. Ware was engaged in research and administrative survey work on Michigan state and local government. He is a member of the Board of Foreign Scholarships by appointment of President Reagan and of Phi Beta Kappa (Lehigh University 1941).

ISBN 0-8447-1380-5

©1986 by the American Enterprise Institute for Public Policy Research, Washington, D.C. All rights reserved. No part of this publication may be used or reproduced in any manner whatsoever without permission in writing from the American Enterprise Institute except in the case of brief quotations embodied in news articles, critical articles, or reviews. The views expressed in the publications of the American Enterprise Institute are those of the authors and do not necessarily reflect the views of the staff, advisory panels, officers, or trustees of AEI.

"American Enterprise Institute" and *AEI* are registered service marks of the American Enterprise Institute for Public Policy Research.

Printed in the United States of America

American Enterprise Institute for Public Policy Research
1150 Seventeenth Street, N.W., Washington, D.C. 20036

Foreword

The American Enterprise Institute is proud to offer a forum for the G. Warren Nutter Memorial Lecture series. The lectures, conducted in cooperation with the Thomas Jefferson Center Foundation, serve as part of the intellectual legacy of an extraordinary individual.

G. Warren Nutter was one of the great conservative intellectuals of his time. He was a scholar and statesman who understood better than most the importance of ideas in the development of public policy. He worked closely with my father, the late William J. Baroody, Sr., to foster new ideas and to create an environment in which the American Enterprise Institute and other public policy research organizations are able to flourish.

Warren taught for many years at the University of Virginia and was chairman of its economics department in the late 1960s. He took leave from 1969 to 1973 to serve as assistant secretary of defense for international security affairs. He was awarded the Defense Department's Distinguished Public Service Medal for his service there. He was a specialist in several aspects of economics: the economics of defense, industrial organization, the Soviet economy, and general microeconomic theory.

I had the privilege of knowing Warren beginning when I was very young, when he would join my father and other scholars at our home for dinner and discussion. Many times in recent years I have looked at the turns public policy has taken and thought back to what Warren Nutter said about the role of government in free societies. He advocated a greater balance between the public and private sectors.

"The question at issue," he wrote, "is not whether Americans should believe in either individualism or collectivism. Neither is adequate to serve by itself as the philosophic foundation of a viable democratic republic. The underlying philosophy must be a mixture of both. But it is critically important which dominates."[1]

He believed individualism was essential to individual liberty, and his life and his teachings were testaments to this idea.

I am personally very pleased to have Richard Ware present the twelfth Nutter Lecture. He is cut from the same cloth as Warren Nutter, William J. Baroody, Sr., and other intellectual pioneers who challenged the prevailing wisdom in the 1950s, 1960s, and 1970s. In good times and bad, their faith in certain bedrock principles never wavered.

In his work with the Earhart Foundation, in his service as Warren Nutter's principal deputy at the Pentagon, and in many other endeavors, Dick Ware was devoted to the important values in life: integrity, excellence, family, and country. This is a man, like Warren Nutter, of substance, of character, of vision.

Bill Baroody Jr.

WILLIAM J. BAROODY, JR.
President
American Enterprise Institute

---

1. G. Warren Nutter, *Political Economy and Freedom: A Collection of Essays*, edited by Jane Couch Nutter (Indianapolis: Liberty Press, 1983), p. 57.

Introduction

John F. Lehman, Jr.
Secretary of the Navy

In introducing me, Bill Baroody, the president of AEI, made a reference to the Navy's "Qaddafi watch." Actually, I came from more perilous waters, dealing with *more* of a threat. I bring you greetings from Senator Phil Gramm, which is why I was a little late.

This is an opportunity I have been looking forward to for a long time because I go way back with Dick Ware. Our relationship started in early 1963 when I, at the recommendation of Vic Milione of the Intercollegiate Studies Institute, took a trip to Detroit to interest Dick in helping us put together a conference at the University of Pennsylvania. At the time it was called the Philadelphia Collegiate Disarmament Conference. When I first presented the idea to Dick, he reacted in a, shall we say, less than enthusiastic fashion until I explained that we wanted to organize a forum to attempt to stem the tide that was running for unilateral disarmament and unilateral initiative in the test ban treaty of 1963. It was only then that he began to listen; and after I had talked a long time, for the first time I heard the wisdom of Richard Ware, which I have been listening to ever since.

Dick is one of those special people who, as those of you who are "Washington junkies" know, exert the really important and beneficial influences over time. They have a sense of history and a feel for the important, as opposed to the unimportant, ripples on the surface. They stay out of the limelight and out of the press, yet they have an influence far beyond their public image. Dick is one such man.

I worked with him for two years on several conferences and published two books as a result, and throughout Dick was my guide. He introduced me to such little-known persons as Ed Feulner and Richard Allen and helped bring us to work together and to write and "do good works" for the cause of a more sensible view of national security policy. He has always been a tremendous catalyst for bringing good people together in a way that facilitates their helping each other. This has been a hallmark of every stage of his service.

During those two years I was in a bit of a quandary: Dick was quietly questioning why I was headed to law school intent on becoming a Philadelphia lawyer. He would get going on how much more the country needed people in public service than it needed those merely chasing lucre. His arguments had the fermentative effect intended, and I ended up going to graduate school, first at the University of Pennsylvania and then at Cambridge University on a Weaver Fellowship and an Earhart Fellowship, which Dick had a major hand in bringing together.

Then, when I came to Washington for the first time, moving in with Ed Feulner thanks to Dick's earlier introduction, whom did I find at the first meeting I attended in the interdepartmental group at the White House but Dick Ware! I watched his performance carefully because I had never viewed him as a government wallah, and I was unsure of how he would operate.

Well, operate he did. For two years I think I saw Dick in the White House basement more than almost anyone else—at the interdepartment group meetings and the Staff Interagency Group meetings, and so forth. One of his hallmarks was the unique way he had of blending differing civilian and military perspectives. He worked as a tremendous catalyst for keeping the uniformed and civilian sides of the Pentagon from becoming polarized. His successful endeavors have since been mentioned to me a number of times, by people in the Navy at the time, many of whom were junior officers then, and by more senior leaders such as Tom Moorer and others who were major beneficiaries of that inestimable catalytic talent that Dick had.

Another of his qualities worth emulating was that he didn't speak very often. But when he did everybody listened attentively, a lesson that I didn't fully grasp at first. Only in the later part of Dick's tenure at Defense and in my current incarnation have I come to understand fully the value of such a strategy.

Of course, since that time, Dick has remained active, again behind the scenes where it counts most—keeping the right people communicating with each other, keeping the issues that are really important on the agenda of people who count, and quietly introducing new ideas and thoughts.

Dick has had a remarkable career. I am sure you all know his educational background—Phi Beta Kappa from Lehigh, a master's degree from Wayne State—so when he was luring people like Ed and me into government service it was not without some considerable experience. If you look at his record of public service—in the Air Force, in the civilian side of the government during World War II, in state government, as a member of boards of directors and advisory boards for Tufts, the Fletcher School, the University of Chicago, charities, and civic groups—you find that all of these groups are major molders of the ethical direction of this country.

So I feel it a great honor to be able to precede him on this podium. I hope I'm not sounding too much like a funeral eulogist, Dick, but I don't get a chance very often to speak your praises. I have, as I have indicated, a personal debt to Dick that continues to this day. He is a source of continuing inspiration to me and to all of us. If it weren't for you, Dick, I would today, instead of being a poor public servant, be a rich Philadelphia lawyer, so I want to thank you very much.

I recall, Dick, shortly after I got back from Cambridge, your saying, "I remember, John, when I first met you, you were a modest, good-humored boy, and now Cambridge has made you insufferable." I hope that was meant in jest, and I would like to ask all of you to join me in welcoming Dick Ware to this distinguished podium.

The Pentagon's Office of International Security Affairs, 1969–1973
or
Two Citizens Go to Washington

Richard A. Ware

Warren Nutter was a unique combination of scholar, teacher, citizen soldier, and public servant. Aside from pride in his family and students, I believe he treasured most his combat infantryman's badge and his doctorate from the University of Chicago, where Frank Knight was his mentor. His qualities also included a quiet sense of humor. At the Edinburgh Festival, just after a stunning performance of a selection from a Verdi opera by a military band of a country not to be identified, he remarked: "If only they had an army to go with it."

I met this man in 1956 or 1957, and our friendship began over a mutual interest in political economy. It ripened when we served together in 1964 on a presidential campaign staff. In 1969 I was one of several who encouraged Warren to accept the Defense Department appointment to the position of assistant secretary of defense for international security affairs. He turned about and nailed me as his principal deputy.

My service in this role proved that a friendship could survive long hours under much stress and strain. Our thoughts and reactions were such that I was comfortable with his instructions, and he never overruled a decision of mine. Our relationship continued through his long illness, including overseas travel to Europe and the Orient. My wife and I share with Jane many treasured memories.

Until now I have not discussed the Pentagon experience of Messrs. Nutter and Ware. I have preferred to honor the combined Yankee humor and advice of Senator Muskie: "Don't speak unless you can improve upon silence." But, in the Spring 1983 issue of *Political Science Quarterly*, an article assigned a low rating to the Office of International Security Affairs (ISA) of the Nixon-Ford years, with special reference to the Laird-Nutter period. The article was developed without contact with me. So I break my Yankee silence to place in this lecture series a modest and partial record of a major interlude in Nutter's professional life. To put it more colorfully, as Frank Knight did, using the words of a Chicago politician: "The time has come to take the bull by the tail and look the situation square in the face."

My text is culled from a valedictory that Mr. Nutter and I prepared upon his departure from E-Ring of the Pentagon. I also drew upon a scattering of notes I recorded at the time. I shall not "modernize" the context to reflect later events.

Permit me first to mention some of the stagecraft and props useful for senior officials beginning a political appointment in Defense. A discussion of a few of the substantive issues that crossed Secretary Nutter's desk will follow. Then I will conclude with observations founded upon a learning experience in public management in a defense environment.

Power and influence in a bureaucracy are determined by the perceptions of others as much as by one's own ability and activity. There are some conditions and symbols of office that furnish a Pentagon newcomer with a headstart in the daily struggle.

Physical facilities create the first impression. An E-Ring office regularly "swept" or "debugged" is a must. Furnishings should include an oversize desk, conference table, sofa, stuffed leather armchairs, coffee table, flags, and one wall covered with a world map. Do not underestimate the power of a safe of closet size and a private latrine, especially one with a shower. Outside it is best to have an assigned car and driver or at least an assigned parking slot at the foot of the steps to a main entrance.

Support personnel are indispensable. Minimum requirements are a military assistant, sometimes known as a "horse holder," and two personal secretaries, one of whom should be a noncareer political appointee. These three assistants create inaccessibility and wire you to meaningful back channels.

A side table display of telephone buttons to be certain every visitor knows you have direct communication upward and downward is a must. Be sure the one from SECDEF (the Secretary of Defense) rings during the first hour you occupy your office. Another telephone, a white one, must be on display to signify inclusion on the White House switchboard. If it ever rings, you have it made. Be sure to be on the switch of the National Military Command Center, both at the office and at your residence, and have a paging device and a car radio.

Valuable miscellaneous items include both a regular White House pass and one from the Joint Chiefs, the latter providing authority to commandeer a helicopter in event of an attack; clearance for the daily intelligence pouch that goes to about two hundred in the government; "open" travel orders; and membership in SECDEF's mess.

With these "badges of office" and assuming a high degree of self-importance, how can one fail? Well, it is easy, but that's an essay for another day.

I recall SECDEF remarking that about one-third of the policy issues crossing his desk daily originated in Nutter's shop. Some had to do with the newly integrated program of military assistance and sales, a program of in excess of $5 billion that took on greater importance under the Nixon Doctrine. This is a complex and seperate subject.

Another such subject is SALT, but ISA did not have principal responsibility. Early in 1969 the deputy secretary decided to treat SALT as a technical rather than a political problem. ISA participated but did not drive the staff work.

I have selected some geographic areas and issues to illustrate ISA's activities during Nutter's stewardship.

East Asia and the Pacific

Leaving aside such policy issues as Korea, the Republic of China and the PRC, and the trust territories of the Pacific, I will take up Vietnam and Japan.

In virtually every significant respect it was necessary to start almost from scratch in working out the program for extricating the United States from Vietnam and for improving and modernizing South Vietnamese forces. Until 1969 there was no focal point within Defense for supervising the effort. The services were devoting their efforts to military operations. They were not preparing the Vietnamese to take over. Secretary of Defense Melvin Laird assigned to ISA the task of overseeing the Vietnamization effort, and he participated through daily meetings with Mr. Nutter and his staff.

ISA proceeded first through a loosely formed coordinating group and then with a Vietnam task force created in November 1969 with Brigadier General George S. Blanchard as director. Manned by selected personnel on temporary duty, its counterpart elements emerged throughout Defense and other agencies. Time-phased planning was undertaken covering all aspects of turning the war over to South Vietnam. As one-half million American forces were withdrawn from active combat, Vietnamese forces were recruited, trained, and equipped.

In large measure this effort was successful, but we did not anticipate withdrawal in 1973 of American logistic support. Those of us involved with the Vietnamization activities always have had concern with what was to follow under the communist "program of reeducation."

There was an economic dimension to Vietnamization that was of special interest to Nutter. Until 1969 little had been done to develop a self-sustaining economy in South Vietnam. The fiscal policy followed was one in which low taxes and high government spending were rewarded with U.S. economic assistance. The policy generated a growing deficit in the balance of payments and a built-in incentive for corruption.

Secretary Laird and Mr. Nutter visited Vietnam in early 1970. In his report to the president SECDEF emphasized that the economic situation was the weakest link and stressed revision of the program of economic assistance in preparing for self-generating growth and stability. This aroused little enthusiasm elsewhere in the government. ISA took the initiative in sponsoring a study by William Ford setting forth an economic strategy for South Vietnam; another by Stephen Enke proposed a course of action to implement that strategy.

To stimulate the U.S. mission a section for economic affairs was established in Military Assistance Command, Vietnam, staffed by military officers who were trained economists. An economic counselor was introduced into the mission, a section of the National Security Council (NSC) staff was charged with reviewing the economic program, and a National Security Decision Memorandum was issued setting forth a new course of action. The South Vietnamese government responded on its own part and succeeded in 1971 in cutting the inflation rate in half. The importance of the economic reforms became evident in the ability of the economy to absorb the shock of the North Vietnamese invasion in 1972 to the extent that less assistance was required in the economic than in the military area.

A tragic problem of the Vietnam War revolved around the treatment of U.S. POWs and the accounting for the missing-in-action. The policy until 1969 had been one of silence on the ground that publicity might worsen the prisoners' conditions. Early in the Nixon presidency SECDEF decided to make the issue public despite strong opposition within the government. A token release of three prisoners assisted in securing the attention of the world. These men were permitted to describe their mistreatment, and from that point on Defense pressed the POW/MIA issue as a humanitarian one. Mr. Nutter chaired the policy committee on the issue and had a special assistant charged with coordinating all action implementing Defense POW policy. These efforts were rewarded when the prisoners were returned home. Questions remain about many, and the issue is not closed. Mr. Nutter and I regretted we could not do more for these men and their families.

Another significant issue in the region had to do with the evolving relationship between the United States and Japan. The accepted government position assumed a special Japanese-American relationship that followed the surrender of the USS *Missouri*. This relationship derived from two fundamentals that disappeared in the late 1960s. First, there was the physical and psychological fact that the United States had been the overwhelming victor. Second, there was the unhindered military presence of the U.S. military on Okinawa. As time passed, the American victory diminished in significance, particularly as the Pacific countries grew in strength. The turning point came with the reversion of Okinawa to Japanese control. This act, for which Japan received a cash supplement, removed a foundation of prime power for the United States and placed a burden on bases in the Philippines and possibly in the trust territories.

There were those who argued that Japan would adhere to the mutual defense treaty and forgo a military effort of any significance; that it would content itself with wielding its power through economic and diplomatic force, all the while supporting and following U.S. leadership in world affairs. The reversion of Okinawa removed a burr in the relationship between the two countries. This relationship will remain stable as long as the United States continues to reassure Japan that it will provide both a nuclear shield and a conventional military presence adequate to safeguard Japanese interests.

Mr. Nutter and a few close associates disagreed with the foregoing rationale. Japan as a sovereign state is bound ultimately to base its policies on its national interests as the Japanese perceive them. The Japanese, sooner or later, will realize or draw the appropriate conclusion on how much dependence they can place on being protected by U.S. military forces. Japanese foreign and military policy (not to mention economic policy) will take on an increasingly independent character. The challenge will be to find means of influencing emerging Japanese power in a direction consistent with U.S. security. The U.S. relationship with Japan must be built upon mutual self-interest within the context of the realities of military and economic power. It cannot be built upon a misconceived sense of friendship and affection.

Europe and NATO

Although I cannot discuss all the problems confronted in this directorate (that is, those associated with Iceland, France, Greece, Turkey, Norway's North Cape, and the Dutch desire for a submarine), NATO should not be overlooked as an alliance that has preserved a general European peace for two generations.

One of the consequences of the Vietnam War was a deterioration of U.S. relations with Europe and particularly with the alliance. By 1969 Vietnam had consumed our military resources as well as the attention of those charged with the conduct of foreign relations. We had degraded our military capabilities in Europe and the Mediterranean to fight in Southeast Asia. We had engaged in other reductions of forces under pressure of the "balance of payments" problems created by the war and inadequate fiscal and financial arrangements to prosecute it. Our attention had been shifted from that part of the world most vital to the defense of the United States.

The degradation and neglect were compounded by a domineering attitude toward our allies. It was slight wonder that there was little enthusiasm among them for any concerted effort at mending fences and building a sounder partnership. The foregoing was reflected in ISA. In addition Defense had ridden roughshod over State in setting some of this policy.

Major staff changes were accomplished to achieve a more cooperative stance with State. SECDEF brought military problems out in the open and then discussed them with candor. Proceeding step by step, it was possible to promote a sense of cooperation and partnership, to expand NATO activities, and to improve the structure of forces. Successful negotiations were held with the French, and groundwork was laid for the eventual membership of Spain in the alliance. The member nations developed a more sophisticated attitude with special reference to the changes necessary because of the parity in strategic nuclear forces attained between the United States and the USSR. The Secretary of Defense cultivated close personal relations with his counterparts of the NATO countries. This was a considerable shift from the prior administration.

For a few moments I want to describe some of the problems in the NATO directorate below the policy level that occasionally enlivened and complicated one's day.

Late one afternoon State delivered to ISA a policy paper setting forth the basis for Spanish base negotiations, including a fallback position for the use of some military assistance funds. Our staff worked until 11:00 that night preparing comments for the deputy secretary and the chairman of the Joint Chiefs to use at a National

Security Council group meeting. This paper was presented to me at 10:10 the next morning for signature and delivery to the deputy secretary by 10:30. Too frequently, neither Secretary Nutter nor I was able to give much thoughtful consideration to a major policy before recommending it to our superiors.

At another time State dispatched a cable to U.S. embassies in Europe having to do with a 10 percent reduction in forces. The principal deputy had approved the contents for Defense, but after his approval someone in State deleted a paragraph, but left in place the deputy's initials. It took several hours to restore calm within the Joint Chiefs and to prepare a follow-up cable.

Sometimes the error of a clerk in records and control has major consequences. Certain information about the storage of nuclear arms was sent to NATO ministers of defense by SECDEF. As sensitive documents, they should have gone by courier. One day they were placed in the wrong outbox and were transmitted by registered mail. The minister of defense of the Federal Republic of Germany reported the lapse to ISA. Life immediately became hectic. We knew that registered mail to at least one NATO capital went through a Warsaw Pact country.

Within an hour after the situation had been reported to the principal deputy he had consulted the security services, created a task force to manage any special problems and recommend corrective procedures, developed a report to SECDEF after having notified his executive officer, reported to Atomic Energy Commission authorities, and briefed the U.S. ambassador to NATO by secure telephone. We had to make sure the registered mail had been delivered in all destination countries and that the material was got back into regular channels without being compromised. The latter required a careful political watch with tight security on knowledge of the incident. The file was successfully closed six months later.

Southwest Asia

This region usually is described as the Middle East and South Asia. In ISA Africa was thrown in for good measure. At the outset of our watch Africa was a part of the Directorate for Inter-American Affairs, and the Indian Ocean was divided among three regions. We believed this did not accord with strategic reality since this ocean is an entity for the control of sea lanes and is used by the Soviet Union to establish a presence.

Insofar as the Indian Ocean is concerned, the single significant accomplishment was support for the establishment of the U.S. communication facility on Diego Garcia. It is not necessary over a decade later to say more.

The Arab-Israeli conflict dominated staff activity, although it was not given a high priority by the White House in the early months of the Nixon administration. Secretary Nutter's considerations of it were guided by three principles. First, the tail should not wag the dog, which is to say that the United States should not permit a condition to arise wherein actions taken by either Israel or its enemies would automatically determine U.S. policy. The United States should maintain sufficient independence to ensure that its foreign policy flows from an American appreciation of its own national interests. Early on we discovered this concept was violated at the working level within our own shop. Israeli intelligence officers could contact ISA personnel directly and independent of the policies governing activities of military attachés. Further, we learned that intelligence elements of one U.S. service had established special relations with counterparts in the Israeli armed forces, entering into agreements and arranging exchanges of information without reference to other components of Defense. This practice was eliminated by the deputy secretary in a special directive.

Second, every effort was to be made to prevent a serious confrontation in the region between the United States and the USSR. Such a confrontation, particularly if it should imply a nuclear showdown, could result in a Cuba in reverse. A careful reading of the realities of the American scene makes it reasonably clear that U.S. military support of Israel is likely to be greatest when least needed and least when most needed.

Third, avoid creating a powder keg likely to lead to a wider conflict. The United States had (in 1969) no enemies among the countries and peoples of the region; Nutter believed it was in our national interest to maintain friendly relations with all states to prevent any oil-rich territory from falling into the hands of another major world power, and that it was also in our interest to maintain a climate sufficiently peaceful to remove the basis for steady Soviet infiltration.

Last, it seemed to us that the Mediterranean should be considered somewhere within the Pentagon as an entity with its own economic, political, cultural, and strategic concerns. We never succeeded in mounting even a study based on such a notion.

Inter-American Affairs

In 1969 individuals in State were allied with some in ISA in an almost messianic mission of social reform in Latin American countries. Essentially, this meant removing the military from positions of authority, with the resultant ascendancy of left-wing forces. Contacts with the military were minimized, and Defense was substantially removed from any role in the formulation of U.S. policy. It was as if there were no national security interests south of the border.

These views also dominated the policy in the Caribbean area where there was an emphasis on promoting independence for all colonial islands, no matter how sparsely populated or how strategically located with respect to the U.S. mainland. Among the efforts to rectify the situation were the visits to Latin America made by Secretary Nutter in late 1971, the first made by an assistant secretary of defense for international security affairs. From then on, trips by senior military and defense officials were scheduled to some part of Latin America.

The case of Chile loomed large during our watch. Many thought this unusual because it is about as distant from Washington as Moscow is. Some urged that if Chile chose communism then the United States should abide by that choice. ISA consistently took the position that it is important to recognize a potentially aggressive totalitarian state as it develops.

We were concerned about the danger to stability in the Western Hemisphere should Chile and Cuba become partners in communism. Chile also is of strategic importance because of (1) its long border with Argentina and other countries, (2) its long coastline with the only three deep-water ports on the west coast, (3) its control of both shores of the Straits of Magellan, and (4) its control of Easter Island in the South Pacific. Fortunately, Chile stepped back from the brink.

ISA managed to hold a strong position on the Panama Canal issue and gave attention to Guantanamo as an outpost. I visited the base to demonstrate the importance we attached to it and to "show the flag" to the 5,000 U.S. military then stationed there.

One should remember that during this time the Soviet Union made its first move toward establishing a naval presence in Cuba, a presence that has continued with far-reaching consequences for the defense of the continental United States, along our South Atlantic perimeter. Even so, a draft paper prepared for the National Security Council gave no attention to a visit of Soviet warships, underplayed the export of revolution from Cuba, and placed the retention of a U.S. base in Cuba in the lowest category.

Strategic Trade and Foreign Military Rights

Among the miscellaneous functions of ISA were those having to do with controls governing trade and technical disclosure with potential adversaries, and the politics in the host countries of overseas military facilities and forces. I will discuss only the former. Under directives from Secretary Laird, ISA formed a rear guard and opposed almost every action that was sought by other departments or allied nations. It made no sense to provide economic and technological information to the Soviet Union without receiving something commensurately valuable in return. In New England this is known as "dickering."

Our staff stood fast in the face of mounting pressure from every quarter of the government. Defense sometimes was overruled, sometimes after a controversy's escalation to the highest level. Important examples included sale of machine tools for the Soviet Kama River truck factory, of French and UK integrated circuit-making machinery to Poland, and of communication equipment to Warsaw Pact nations. "Diplomatic gain" was the usual reason given.

Bureaucratic games were played. In one case an American firm applied for an export license to sell $21 million worth of machine tools to the Soviet Union to produce truck gears. State and Commerce told NSC staff that Defense would agree, and NSC staff told Defense staff people that the White House wanted approval. ISA staff went along but were overruled despite pleas from Commerce. Secretary Laird agreed, and Defense voted "no," forcing the decision to the president. By the close of business on February 6, 1970, word was received that the president had upheld the Secretary of Defense. On March 27, 1970, State cabled the U.S. Embassy in Moscow that the "cases remain under review."

In a recent book by Ambassador U. Alexis Johnson there is a reference to such problems.[1] After commenting that Warren Nutter had none of a predecessor's "flair for making decisions and getting things done," Ambassador Johnson went on to say that he was forced "to take up an unusually heavy volume of business between State and Defense with the Deputy Secretary of Defense." He explains that "Though many of those issues on which we collaborated were insignificant and should have been settled at lower levels, such as minor export licensing matters . . ." Translated, this suggests that ISA was an obstructionist to sound national policy on strategic trade matters. I respectfully disagree.

The French newspaper *Le Monde* has been quoted as saying a KGB document shows the USSR gets 61.5 percent of its industrial secrets from the United States, 10.5 percent from West Germany, and 7.5 percent from the United Kingdom.[2]

The assistant secretary and his principal deputy were subjected to a clinical learning experience in public management. The office they headed is most easily described as the Pentagon's "little State Department." As might be expected Foggy Bottom did not relish a rival activity, especially one run by "amateurs" in a military setting.

Upon assuming office Mr. Nutter was given a twofold charge by Secretary Laird: conduct ISA's affairs with the lowest possible profile within and outside the arena of government, and do all possible to prevent a wedge from being driven between State and Defense. I suggest that the first part of this charge hardly was a prescription for being perceived as an effective bureaucrat.

ISA had principal responsibility for coordinating all activities in DOD concerned with the international aspects of defense, and for being the principal contact on these matters with other government agencies. This meant ISA coordinated with the Joint Chiefs of Staff in developing the position of the Secretary of Defense in the formal NSC structure and process initiated by the Nixon administration. This included the responsibilities of the Washington Special Actions Group for the policies in a variety of crisis or sensitive situations.

In 1969 it was reasonably clear that our immediate predecessors had assumed a personal control over many activities. Such details in Vietnam as bombing targets consumed attention to the neglect of guidance and leadership in other areas of political-military affairs. There was more concern with the influence they could be seen wielding on policy formulation than with providing staff support to the Secretary of Defense and contributing to an overall executive branch policy. Their style was freewheeling and flamboyant.

We found relations between the Office of the Secretary and the Joint Chiefs to have deteriorated to the point that cooperative effort was the exception. The basic cause was a presumption that the military was misguided, ill informed, and most of the time wrong. Each side considered the other an adversary. Trench lines were everywhere, and there was almost constant cannonading in the corridors. It was not an atmosphere in which knowledge and judgment could be brought to bear properly on serious defense issues.

The management problem was one of shaping an organization independent of the day-to-day decisions of a single individual and recasting it into an important element of support for the president and the secretary. This task required a change in style with a focus on getting the job done instead of getting credit for it, on cooperating with other parts of the executive branch, and on forming a relation with the military based on mutual respect.

The NSC process facilitated good working relations within the department, particularly between the Office of the Secretary and the Joint Chiefs. There was teamwork in preparing coordinated defense positions, and this carried over into other activities. NSC demands on the department during 1969–1970, however, were so overburdening that staff was tied up in producing papers of low quality at best.

Perhaps this was by design to free the White House to take on and decide issues of its choice.

The foregoing experience produced some suggestions useful for assuming control of a policy shop in Defense in a new administration differing sharply from its predecessor. First, and no later than when sworn into office, be sure all positions held by political or noncareer appointees are vacant. Fill the vacancies quickly. Meanwhile continuity will be assured by career military and civilian personnel. Second, identify those who have moved from noncareer slots back to permanent grades in the classified service in order to better understand their policy concerns and interests.

Third, by reclassifying positions or establishing new ones, move out of the direct line of responsibility and command those who determined policy under the previous administration. Fourth, have at least one person in the front office with knowledge of the bureaucracy and its functioning. Equally important, have someone with political know-how.

Fifth, identify all those who control the flow of information, making sure of their loyalty to the new administration. The president, cabinet, and subcabinet officers learn only from information filtered by staff. Sixth, the front office should control budget and personnel matters. Mr. Nutter changed the relationship of the assistant secretary and his principal deputy so the latter could act for the former or be his alternate at any time. As a part of this arrangement the principal deputy controlled those functions necessary to maintain a responsive staff, including recruitment and assignment of personnel, travel and leave, security violations, etc.

I turn now to some illustrations and special problems.

Personnel records were a mess. It took from mid-March to mid-July 1969 to determine the number of slots in ISA, the number of employees aboard, and who was assigned to do what. Only a threat to have a "dress right dress" lineup in the corridor of everyone—general to clerk—produced the requisite information. We found ISA personnel at the White House and elsewhere on informal assignments who were charged to Defense. Contracts with "think tanks" provided staff persons at costs frequently double a government salary. Military personnel were selected and assigned by subordinate offices without regard to overall requirements.

Throughout such trying experiences the military personnel assigned to ISA facilitated efforts for change and improvement. They are accustomed to a new skipper coming aboard and they responded. Furthermore, the 1969 change in command was welcomed by most career officers and by some dedicated civilians. These career staff proved to be strongly motivated, competent, and willing to work long hours.

Secretaries Laird and Packard always moved for the reduction of administrative costs, and ISA cooperated by cutting staff at least 10 percent. Such reductions in force have a price, however. Those with seniority are retained, making it impossible to keep newer employees of superior competence or to bring in new people more responsive to policy.

It seemed sensible to develop an all-inclusive list of consultants. The process got under way in May 1969 with the selection of forty-six. Fourteen months later six had been cleared. By April 1971, forty specialists were available, with an additional three by 1973. This frustrating experience did not end there. We then found that senior policy people in our own shop, and who were our own appointees, did not call on this talent bank. Special efforts were made to set up seminars, staff conferences, and "A" and "B" teams, but they were not taken seriously unless the assistant secretary or the principal deputy participated. There was the notion that those on the "inside" have a monopoly of information and wisdom.

ISA must relate to a variety of other departments and agencies of which the Department of State is the most important. Even though instructed to work cooperatively with our colleagues there, differences in respective approaches led inevitably to institutional differences in policies, thus underscoring why the president needs the advice of both departments to project foreign policy.

State, for example, is most comfortable when policy is loosely defined, thereby providing the greatest flexibility for diplomacy. Defense is most comfortable when policy is strictly defined, thereby providing a firm base for military plans and operations. State is inclined to postpone every possible decision because circumstances may change or the problem may go away. In military affairs decisions cannot be deferred; if an army or fleet is to be provisioned and moved, precise logistical decisions must be made. Last, State sometimes is inclined to use defense assets, although Defense finds the means and also better appreciates the limitations.

Fundamental to all national security decisions is the quality of intelligence. ISA was one of the largest consumers and had little to say about levying requirements on the community. The staff suprisingly had few comments on the adequacy of the intelligence received. In the front office, we were concerned after listening to a briefing on the burden of military spending on the Soviet Union that implied some of the same conclusions and theories extant in 1950–1955. We were informed on the same occasion both that the Soviets had no intention of more than maintaining a balance with U.S. strategic power and that the United States had no precise knowledge of Soviet weapon technology.

We made three generalizations about the U.S. intelligence function in 1973 that may remain valid. First, it is based on a "mirror image"; that is, we assume another power or adversary will react to the United States as we react to that power,[3] and inadequate attention was given to the unpredictable or to the acts of irrational leaders. Pearl Harbor and the Cuban missile crisis are examples. Second, analysis and evaluation of events tilted toward support of policies already decided. Third, post-mortems seldom were held to evaluate intelligence performance.

There had been hope that a series of special research studies could be produced using intelligence sources and our consulting panel. Already mentioned was consideration of the Mediterranean as an economic and strategic unit. Another could have dealt with Soviet intentions in the world's "hot spots" or with Soviet basing plans as the Soviets saw them.

This recitation of an assortment of administrative trials and tribulations cannot be complete, but perhaps I have conveyed some of the flavor for the challenges two citizens found after reporting for duty on the fourth floor of the Pentagon's E-Ring.

Conclusion

Most important of all was the dedication and know-how we encountered among a large percentage of our civilian and military comrades. The Republic is fortunate to have a corps of loyal servants.

From relationships established with employees in policy and substantive positions, I observed that all "doves" were not civilians, and all "hawks" were not in the military. Neither were all "politicians" found only among the political appointees.

The last, the political appointees, play an essential role in bringing new perspectives and policies to policy determination and implementation plus a degree of independence of judgment, especially if they are on leave from a nonfederal position. Those whose economic well-being depends upon political acceptance of their decisions, or who wish to ascend the ladder to more power, do not have this independence of judgment or do not choose to use it. This is a "glitch" not to be minimized.

Long-range planning—the lack thereof—was a disappointment. It should have been a major ISA function, but it was poorly performed before 1969 and was no better upon our departure in 1973. ISA was tagged with the longest and shortest fuses in Defense. Operational and urgent problems preempted resources.

General Andrew Goodpaster once described to Secretary Nutter and me a small strategic planning group. Working under General Marshall and consisting of Colonels Bonisteel, Goodpaster, and Rusk, the group was given free rein to think about the future. We were not successful in replicating such an effort.

There were a few successes, if I may be excused for mentioning them.

ISA had a role in putting the Vietnamization program on track so that 550,000 American military personnel could be withdrawn without major losses. It is unfortunate that future decisions in Washington canceled what might otherwise have prevented death and misery for millions and handed over to the Soviet Union some excellent military bases.

The ISA role in securing the return of the POWs furnished satisfaction, and the key island outpost of Diego Garcia has proven itself. Some fine officers and civilians were trained for greater responsibility. Many rose to high rank in their services or in the State Department. The principal deputy was totally immersed in public affairs and national security matters that strengthened his work as a foundation manager over subsequent years.

Secretary Nutter, with his logical and perceptive mind, retentive memory, and sense of the Republic's well-being, experienced a four-year postdoctoral program of training for responsibility at a higher level. The citizens of this nation are the poorer for the too early loss of Warren Nutter's capabilities and his loyalty to country.

I thank the Thomas Jefferson Center Foundation, the American Enterprise Institute, and you patient listeners for indulging my desire to enter these remarks in the record.

Notes

1. U. Alexis Johnson, *The Right Hand of Power* (Englewood Cliffs, N.J.: Prentice Hall, Inc., 1984), p. 523.

2. *U.S. News & World Report*, Sept. 30, 1985, p. 32.

3. In commenting on the Cuban missile crisis this is phrased more elegantly by Walter Laqueur in *A World of Secrets* (New York: Basic Books, 1985), p. 169: "The primary reason seems to be that the estimators were inclined to foist American constructs about nuclear strategy on Soviet policy and to attribute American conceptions of rationality in policy making to the Soviet leadership."